# SIMPLE MACHINES
# Wheels and Axles

by Kay Manolis

BELLWETHER MEDIA • MINNEAPOLIS, MN

Note to Librarians, Teachers, and Parents:

**Blastoff! Readers** are carefully developed by literacy experts and combine standards-based content with developmentally appropriate text.

**Level 1** provides the most support through repetition of high-frequency words, light text, predictable sentence patterns, and strong visual support.

**Level 2** offers early readers a bit more challenge through varied simple sentences, increased text load, and less repetition of high-frequency words.

**Level 3** advances early-fluent readers toward fluency through increased text and concept load, less reliance on visuals, longer sentences, and more literary language.

**Level 4** builds reading stamina by providing more text per page, increased use of punctuation, greater variation in sentence patterns, and increasingly challenging vocabulary.

**Level 5** encourages children to move from "learning to read" to "reading to learn" by providing even more text, varied writing styles, and less familiar topics.

Whichever book is right for your reader, Blastoff! Readers are the perfect books to build confidence and encourage a love of reading that will last a lifetime!

This edition first published in 2010 by Bellwether Media, Inc.

Library of Congress Cataloging-in-Publication Data
Manolis, Kay.
  Wheels and axles / by Kay Manolis.
     p. cm. – (Blastoff! readers. Simple machines)
  Includes bibliographical references and index.
  Summary: "Simple text, full color photographs, and illustrations introduce beginning readers to the basic principles of wheels and axles. Developed by literary experts for students in grades 2 through 5"–Provided by publisher.
  ISBN 978-1-60014-347-2 (hardcover : alk. paper)
  1. Wheels–Juvenile literature. 2. Axles–Juvenile literature. I. Title.

TJ181.5.M35 2010
621.8–dc22                          2009008274

# Contents

# What Is a Wheel and Axle?

Have you ever ridden a skateboard? Skateboards have **wheels and axles**. Wheels and axles help skateboards roll smoothly. A wheel and axle is a **simple machine**. A simple machine has few or no moving parts. Wheels and axles help move people and objects from one place to another. This is called doing **work**.

**fun fact**

Skateboard axles are called trucks.

Simple machines make work easier. You use **force** when you do work. Force causes objects to start moving, stop moving, or change direction. You use force when you throw or catch a ball. The amount of force you use is called **effort**. Simple machines reduce the amount of effort you need to do work.

# How Wheels and Axles Work

**wheel**

**axle**

A wheel and axle has two parts that work together. The larger part is the wheel. The axle is a smaller wheel or rod attached to the wheel. The wheel and axle always turn together. Since the wheel is larger, it always moves a greater distance than the smaller axle.

When you turn the wheel, the axle moves a short distance, but with more force. This happens when you open a door.

It also happens when you turn a water faucet on or off. One turn of the handle makes the axle open or close a water valve.

When you turn the axle, the wheel moves a longer distance, but with less force. This happens when you ride a bicycle. Bicycle pedals are attached to axles. When you press down on the pedals, the wheels turn.

Wheels and axles make it easier to move
objects. Have you ever tried pushing a
heavy box on the ground? The bottom
of the box scrapes the ground.

This kind of scraping is called **friction**. Wheels and axles roll so they reduce friction. It is easier to push a box on a cart when it is on wheels and axles than when it is on the ground.

wheels

# Examples of Wheels and Axles

There are many kinds of wheels and axles. A screwdriver is a wheel and axle. The handle is the wheel and the shaft is the axle. You apply force by turning the handle, or wheel, end of the screwdriver. The axle end, or shaft, moves at the same time. This turning force is called **torque**.

**Gears** are wheels and axles with grooved edges called teeth. The teeth are designed to fit together so that as one gear turns, it causes another to move.

Sometimes large gears are attached to small gears. The large gears turn at a slower rate than the small gears, but with greater force. Gears help bicycle and car wheels turn faster or slower.

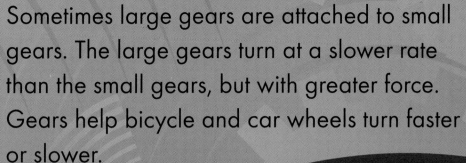

## fun fact

A gear train is a group of two or more gears that work together. The gear that is turned first is called the driver.

# Wheels, Axles, and Complex Machines

Wheels and axles are often parts of **complex machines**. A complex machine is made of two or more simple machines that work together. Many amusement park rides are complex machines that use wheels and axles. One of the tallest rides is the Ferris wheel. A Ferris wheel is a wheel and axle that you can ride!

## fun fact

The tallest Ferris wheel on Earth is called the Singapore Flyer. It is 541 feet (165 meters) tall.

# Glossary

**complex machine**—a machine made of two or more simple machines that work together

**effort**—the amount of force needed to move an object from one place to another

**force**—a push or pull that causes an object to move, change its direction, or stop moving

**friction**—the scraping that happens when an object rubs against another surface

**gear**—a wheel and axle that has grooved edges called teeth

**simple machine**—a machine that has few or no moving parts

**torque**—a force that turns or twists

**wheel and axle**—a simple machine that is made up of a smaller wheel or shaft, called the axle, that is inserted into a larger wheel; both parts always turn together.

**work**—to move an object from one place to another

# To Learn More

**AT THE LIBRARY**

Douglas, Lloyd G. *What Is a Wheel and Axle?* New York, N.Y.: Children's Press, 2002.

Gardner, Robert. *Sensational Science Projects with Simple Machines.* Berkley Heights, N.J.: Enslow, 2006.

Hewitt, Sally. *Machines We Use.* New York, N.Y.: Children's Press, 1998.

**ON THE WEB**

Learning more about simple machines is as easy as 1, 2, 3.

1. Go to www.factsurfer.com.

2. Enter "simple machines" into the search box.

3. Click the "Surf" button and you will see a list of related Web sites.

With factsurfer.com, finding more information is just a click away.

# Index

The images in this book are reproduced through the courtesy of: Marek Tihelka, front cover; Tomasz Trojanowski, pp. 4-5; Joos Mind / Getty Images, pp. 6-7; Jon Eppard, pp. 8-9; silverlining56, p. 10; Yuris, p. 11; Robert Laberge, pp. 12-13; Image Source / Getty Images, p. 14; Glowimages RM / Age Fotostock, p. 15; Mehmet Ali Ciftci, pp. 16-17; yuyangc, p. 18; kkgas, p. 19; Steve Geer, pp. 20-21.